Oh Where, Oh Where?

A Red Fox Book

Published by Random House Children's Books
20 Vauxhall Bridge Road, London SW1V 2SA

A division of The Random House Group Ltd
London Melbourne Sydney Auckland
Johannesburg and agencies throughout the world

3 5 7 9 10 8 6 4 2

First published in Great Britain by The Bodley Head Children's Books 1998

Red Fox edition 2001

Printed and bound in Singapore

THE RANDOM HOUSE GROUP Limited Reg. No. 954009

www.randomhouse.co.uk

ISBN 0 09 926282 7

Oh Where, Oh Where?

JOHN PRATER

RED FOX

Oh where, oh where

has my little bear gone?

Oh where, oh

where can he be?

With his soft little

paws, and big wet nose,

Oh where, oh

where is he?

Oh where, oh where

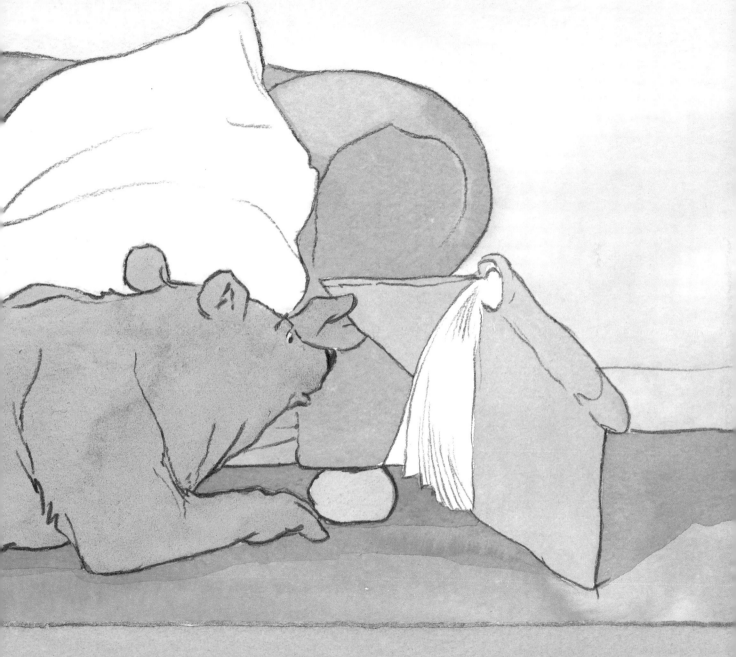

has my little bear gone?

Oh where, oh

where can he be?

With his waggly ears

and twinkly eyes,

Oh where, oh

where is he?

Oh there, oh there

...s my dear little bear.

Come over

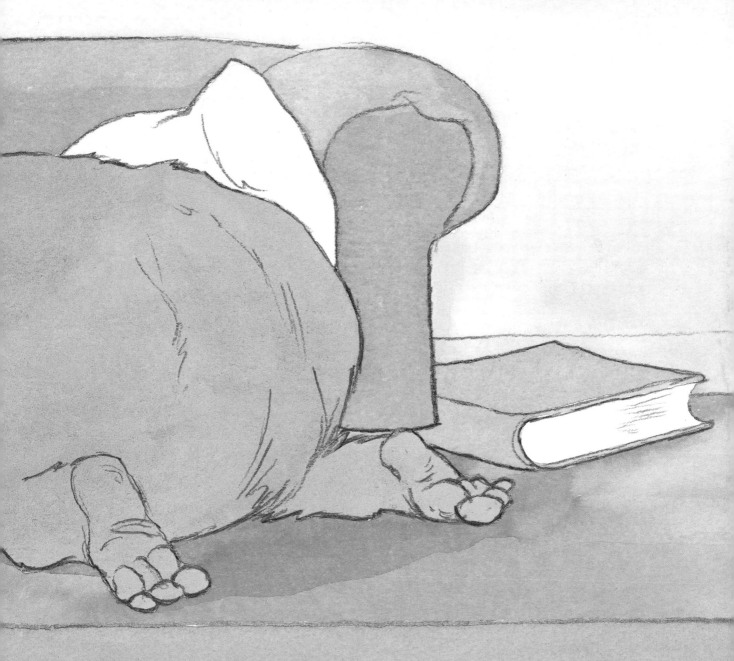

here to me.

A kiss and a cuddle

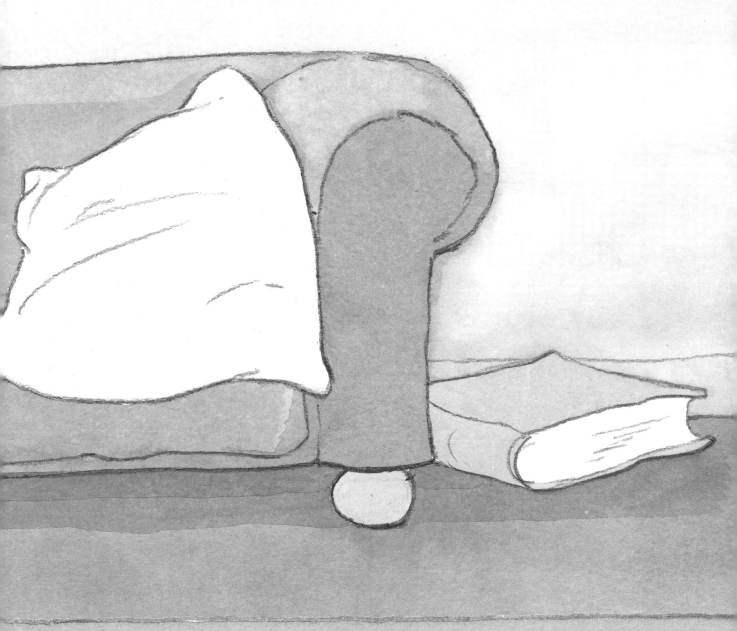

need from you,

Before we

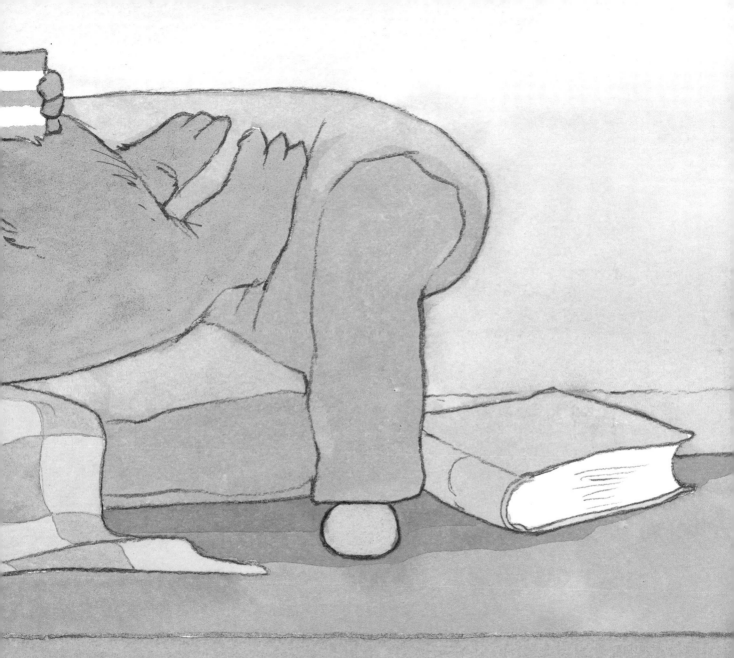

nave our tea.